W9-ASN-959

IF EXTINCT BEASTS CAME TO LIFE

PREHISTORIC ANCESTORS OF MODERN ANIMALS

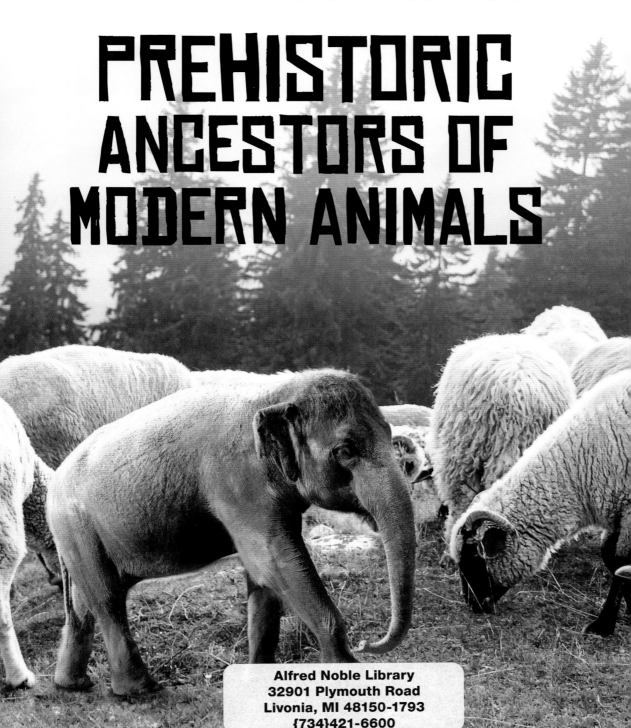

Thanks to the creative team:
Senior Editor: Alice Peebles
Consultant: Neil Clark
Fact Checker: Kate Mitchell
Design: www.collaborate.agency

Hungry Tomato™
A division of Lerner Publishing Group, Inc.
241 First Avenue North
Minneapolis, MN 55401 USA

For reading levels and more information, look up this title at www.lernerbooks.com.

Main body text set in Franklin Gothic Book 11/12.
Typeface provided by International Typeface Corp.

Library of Congress Cataloging-in-Publication Data

The Cataloging-in-Publication Data for *Prehistoric Ancestors of Modern Animals* is on file at the Library of Congress.
ISBN 978-1-5124-0632-0 (lib. bdg.)
ISBN 978-1-5124-1159-1 (pbk.)
ISBN 978-1-5124-0906-2 (EB pdf)

Manufactured in the United States of America
1-39305-21142-8/31/2016

IF EXTINCT BEASTS CAME TO LIFE

PREHISTORIC ANCESTORS OF MODERN ANIMALS

by Matthew Rake
Illustrated by Simon Mendez

HUNGRY TOMATO.

CONTENTS

PREHISTORIC ANCESTORS

Can you imagine what the world would be like if prehistoric animals came back to life? Well, you are about to find out. What's so bizarre is that some of these animals will look familiar to you: they are the ancestors of modern mammals, reptiles, and insects. And they have crash-landed in a location near you. So watch out—it's as if they had not gone extinct after all!

All life started in the sea—and there were some pretty weird creatures 505 million years ago. *Hallucigenia* (*right*) had long, thin legs and spines on its back. In time, some creatures moved out of the water to live on land.

The oldest known land animal is a millipede from 428 million years ago. In time these crawlers grew to 7 feet, 6 inches (2.3 meters) long! Good thing they didn't fly—they might have collided with **dragonflies the size of modern birds of prey**.

Hallucigenia

Eoraptor

When they evolved 240–230 million years ago, ***dinosaurs were about the size of turkeys***. One of the first was *Eoraptor* (*left*). It was only 3 feet, 3 inches (1 m) long (much of which was tail) and weighed about the same as a dachshund. With abundant food and oxygen, though, dinosaurs grew and grew, and came to dominate the planet for about 160 million years.

While dinosaurs ruled, most mammals were the size of shrews, simply to avoid being eaten by those hungry carnivores. But after the dinosaurs died out, *many mammals became massive—and so did reptiles.* Did you know that a rodent the size of a buffalo and a snake longer than a bus once roamed the Earth? What if you saw them rampaging around your world? They're not likely to be as nicely behaved as a pet guinea pig or lizard!

Dwarf elephant

Sometimes it worked the other way. Imagine an African elephant towering over its tiny ancestor, the island-dwelling dwarf elephant (*left*). This little guy would even have looked small next to the well-named *elephant bird, standing 10 feet (3 m) tall* (*below*).

What would it be like to bring these (and other) animal ancestors back to life in all their weird and wonderful glory—and scariness? If you've got the courage, read on . . .

. . . and be prepared for some truly bizarre and spine-tingling encounters between modern creatures and prehistoric beasts.

Elephant bird

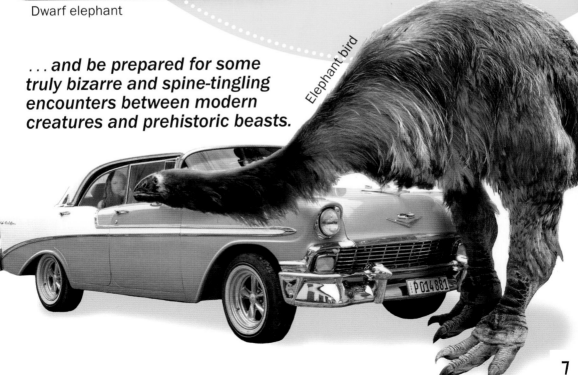

MONSTER SNAKE

TITANOBOA

Something's hissssssing. And it's sssslipped through the water and ssssslithered into a pool where hippos are hanging out. Yes, it's a snake all right, but not just any snake. It's 48 feet (14.6 m) of pure muscle—longer than five ping-pong tables put end to end.

You wouldn't think a massive hippo would be troubled by a snake, no matter how big. But this is *Titanoboa*. It's going for the hippo's neck, and it's ready to puncture the hide with its long, sharp teeth. And if you think that even *Titanoboa* would not be able to get its mouth around a hippo's neck, remember that a snake's lower jaws can unhinge into two halves.

Titanoboa's teeth were probably curved so that prey couldn't pull away. With its grip steady, it could then coil its immensely powerful body around the hippo. This would shut off the blood supply to the hippo's vital organs, such as its heart and brain. So *Titanoboa* would literally be squeezing the life out of this poor old hippo.

TITANOBOA
PRONOUNCED
Tie-tan-oh-BO-ah

LIVED
South America,
60 million–58 million
years ago

LENGTH
Up to 48 feet (14.6 m)

WEIGHT
About 1.25 tons
(1.13 metric tons)

WALKING JAWS

Titanoboa's jaws not only came apart but could also move forward separately. So it would have "walked" its jaws along the body of the hippo to swallow it. Its curved teeth could grip on one side while the other half of the jaw moved forward until the whole hippo vanished!

DISSOLVED BY ACID

Once the hippo had been swallowed by *Titanoboa*, it would be dissolved by acids in the snake's stomach. The actual kill might take a matter of minutes, but the digestion would take days!

MIGHTY RODENT
JOSEPHOARTIGASIA

The capybara is a large rodent that can grow up to 4 feet, 4 inches (1.34 m) long. Fortunately you're unlikely to meet it beause it lives in the Amazon rainforests. Now can you imagine a capybara relative as big as a buffalo—the largest rodent ever? It went by the name *Josephoartigasia,* and it used its huge incisor teeth with the same force as a tiger. It's really the last thing you'd want to see in the garden . . .

At the moment at least, these *Josephoartigasia* seem happy rooting around the trash and having a relaxing swim in the pool. But it won't be long before they are inside the house. Rodents can chew their way through brick, wood, concrete, and even a 0.4-inch-thick (1 centimeter) sheet of metal. So just imagine how easily *Josephoartigasia* could break into a house with those incisors!

BIG HEAD

Josephoartigasia's skull was 21 inches (53 cm) long—much bigger than a lion's or tiger's. And its incisor teeth measured 12 inches (30 cm)!

JOSEPHOARTIGASIA

PRONOUNCED
Joe-SEPH-oh-artig-AH-see-ah

LIVED
South America, 4 million–2 million years ago

LENGTH
10 feet (3 m)

WEIGHT
2,200 pounds (1,000 kilograms)

THE LIZARD OF AUS

MEGALANIA

Imagine waking up and finding this vicious creature tapping at your bedroom window! It's a *Megalania*, the largest land-based lizard known. It lived in Australia until humans moved there some 50,000–40,000 years ago. And it probably ate the large marsupial mammals that roamed the Outback in those days. These included weighty wombats, such as *Diprotodon*, and colossal kangaroos, such as *Procoptodon*. At the same time, it would have had to look out for the marsupial lion *Thylacoleo* and the crocodile *Quinkana*, which lived on the land and was about the same size as *Megalania*.

This *Megalania* looks like it's after a meal. It smelled by flicking out its forked tongue, and it can definitely tell there is something tasty inside the house. Scientists think it had venom glands loaded with deadly poison, just like modern Komodo dragons. So when *Megalania*'s teeth tore the flesh of its prey, it would also inject venom. This would paralyze the victim's muscles and stop the wound from healing. So a word of advice for everyone in that house: get back inside and lock all the doors and windows!

MEGALANIA
PRONOUNCED
Meg-ah-LANE-ee-ah

LIVED
Southeastern Australia, 2 million–50,000 years ago

LENGTH
18–23 feet (5.5–7 m)

WEIGHT
2.1 tons (1.9 metric tons)

VICIOUS TAIL

Megalania did not just use its tail to help it stand up. Scientists think *Megalania*'s tail was also a lethal weapon for knocking out and injuring prey. The largest modern lizard, the Komodo dragon, uses its tail in exactly the same way.

HUMONGOUS HEDGEHOG

DEINOGALERIX

In several parts of the world, hedgehogs are becoming rarer and rarer. So if you found one while raking a pile of leaves, you'd probably be happy to see it.

You might not feel the same way if you found *Deinogalerix*. This hedgehog was as big as a dog. And it looked truly bizarre. For a start, it did not have quills. What's more, it had a long, thin, cone-shaped head; small, pointy ears; and an exceptionally long tail. There would be nothing to worry about, though. Scientists think this curious creature mainly ate invertebrates—small animals without backbones—such as beetles, dragonflies, crickets, and possibly even snails. Some of the larger species, like this one, may have also hunted small mammals, reptiles, and birds.

DEINOGALERIX
PRONOUNCED
Dye-no-GAL-eriks
LIVED
Gargano, Italy,
10 million–5 million
years ago
LENGTH
Up to 2 feet (60 cm)
WEIGHT
Up to 10 pounds (4.5 kg)

ISLAND LIFE

How did this hedgehog get so big? *Deinogalerix* lived on what was then an island, now the Gargano region of Italy. Island species sometimes grow much larger than their mainland relatives because they often don't have many competitors for food and are not preyed on by large animals.

GIANT BEAVERS
CASTOROIDES

Beavers are truly amazing creatures. They build dams on rivers to give protection from predators such as coyotes, wolves, and bears, and to provide easy access to food. And in the middle of the still water created by the dam, they make lodges from sticks, mud, and rocks. Here, they sleep, eat, and bring up their young (known as kits).

Beavers are the architects, engineers, and landscape designers of the animal world. And they do all the hard work themselves. They drag logs along mudslides and float them along canals to put them in place. With their sharp incisor teeth, they can fell trees 3 feet, 9 inches (1.15 m) in diameter.

And modern beavers are only 2–3 feet (60–90 cm) long. Now imagine what a beaver almost four times bigger could do. This dam is being built by giant beavers known as *Castoroides*. They lived in North America until about 10,000 years ago. It looks as if they are not satisfied with logs—you clearly need a car for a state-of-the-art dam.

CASTOROIDES

PRONOUNCED
Kass-tor-OY-deez

LIVED
Woodlands of
North America,
3 million–10,000
years ago

LENGTH
Up to 8 feet (2.5 m)

WEIGHT
198–276 pounds
(90–125 kg)

BIG RODENTS

Castoroides is the largest rodent ever known in North America. The only rodents known to be bigger are *Phoberomys* and *Josephoartigasia* (*see page 10*), both of which lived in South America.

SMALL WONDERS

DWARF ELEPHANTS

Can you imagine elephants that you can pat on the head like a dog? No, we are not talking baby elephants. These are dwarf elephants, which grew to only about 3 feet, 3 inches (1 m) tall. Until about 10,000 years ago, they lived on islands in the Mediterranean Sea, including Cyprus, Malta, Crete, Sicily, and Sardinia.

So how did they arrive on these islands? Well, the climate has changed a lot in the last 2–3 million years, and this has caused sea levels to vary. When sea levels were low, elephants could reach the islands from Africa and Asia. Once sea levels rose again, though, they would often be stranded there.

Okay, but how did the elephants get so small—and, let's face it, cute? Perhaps only the small elephants survived when drought hit the islands. Also, there was no need for elephants to be large. In Africa, the elephant's huge size puts off lions and other predators from attacking them. But on the islands there were no big predators. There are not many predators in this field either. The dwarf elephants seem to feel at home here, enjoying life with a flock of sheep.

DWARF ELEPHANTS

LIVED
Islands in the
Mediterranean Sea,
2.5 million–10,000
years ago

LENGTH
5 feet–7 feet, 6 inches
(1.5–2.3 m)

WEIGHT
400–500 pounds
(180–225 kg)

BALANCING ACT

If you put one fully grown modern African elephant on one side of a huge weighing scale, you would need about ten dwarf elephants on the other side to balance it.

DEADLY DRAGONFLY

MEGANEURA

To you, dragonflies might seem like small, frail creatures. But to insects, they are pretty ruthless hunters. Midges and mosquitoes, butterflies and moths, mayflies and damselflies all end up as dinner for dragonflies.

Dragonflies hunt on the wing, using their sharp eyesight and strong flying skills to chase down their prey. To kill, the dragonfly usually bites its victim on the head then carries it in its legs to a perch where it will remove the wings and eat the prey, head first.

Luckily, dragonflies in Europe and North America are only 3 inches (8 cm) long, with a 4.7-inch (12 cm) wingspan. But what if they had the wingspan of a small hawk? Well, meet *Meganeura*, the giant dragonfly that lived in the Carboniferous period 300 million years ago. Like modern dragonflies, it probably ate insects, but, given its massive size, it may have also had a taste for small amphibians, millipedes, centipedes, and even the odd reptile. These days it would have even more choice, including small mammals like this rat—whose future really isn't looking too good right about now . . .

MEGANEURA

PRONOUNCED
Meg-ah-NEW-rah

LIVED
Western Europe,
300 million years ago

WINGSPAN
26–30 inches (65–75 cm)

SUPERSIZED INSECTS

Why did *Meganeura* grow so big? Scientists think the size of insects depends on how much oxygen there is in the atmosphere. These days, the oxygen content of the atmosphere is about 21%, but 300 million years ago it was 35%.

SHAKE A LEG
ARTHROPLEURA

Can you imagine coming home after a hard day to be greeted by two alligator-sized millipedes? These millipedes, which seem to have made themselves at home, are *Arthropleura*. They lived in the Carboniferous period more than 300 million years ago. Scientists think they grew so big because there was lots of oxygen in the atmosphere. There were also no big predators living on land for *Arthropleura* to deal with. (The big predators were all in the sea!)

Scientists aren't completely sure what these giants ate. If *Arthropleura* had been a carnivore, it would have needed strong, hard mouthparts, and these fossilize well. But none have ever been found, so scientists think it was probably a herbivore.

So whoever lives in this house need not be too alarmed. The *Arthropleura* aren't after them—the bizarre visitors probably just want a quick munch at the fruit bowl or the house plants!

ARTHROPLEURA
PRONOUNCED
Ar-throw-PLOO-rah

LIVED
Eastern North America and Western Europe, 355 million–300 million years ago

LENGTH
Up to 7 feet, 6 inches (2.3 m)

END TO END
The biggest millipedes of today, such as *Archispirostreptus gigas* of East Africa, reach only around 12 inches (30 cm) long. You would need to put seven or eight of these end to end to match the length of *Arthropleura*.

STRETCH YOUR LEGS
Like many modern millipedes, *Arthropleura* might have eaten dead plant matter. So maybe these two should see if there's a compost heap in the garden. It would be a chance for them to stretch their legs— all forty of them!

DOG VERSUS FROG

BEELZEBUFO

Watch out, there's a Beelzebufo around! And it doesn't look like it's in a good mood. This amphibian, also known as the giant devil frog, was the size of a beach ball and lived at the time of the dinosaurs. It was probably a nasty sit-and-wait predator that gobbled up just about anything that passed by, including luckless lizards, misfortunate mammals, and even day-old dinosaurs.

Today, however, it looks as if it might be snapping at more than it can chew. At 88 pounds (40 kg), a German shepherd is almost 10 times as heavy as this frog. But our frog is not backing off. It has sharp teeth, powerful jaws, and a mouth almost 12 inches (30 cm) wide.

The frog probably won't make a very tasty meal anyway. It has shell-like armor on its back, which may have allowed it to burrow underground to cool down. Or maybe the armor protected it from dinosaurs—and if it worked with dinosaurs, it will probably work with passing German shepherds, too.

BEELZEBUFO

PRONOUNCED
Bee-el-zee-BOO-foe

LIVED
Madagascar,
70 million
years ago

LENGTH
16 inches (41 cm)

WEIGHT
10 pounds (4.5 kg)

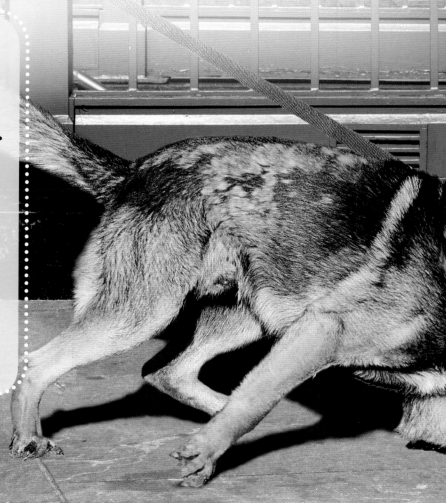

PAC-MAN FROGS

Living descendants of the devil frog are called Ceratophyrines. They have been nicknamed Pac-Man frogs because their big mouth and round body shape resemble the 1980s video game character, Pac-Man.

RUFFLING FEATHERS
ELEPHANT BIRD

Anyone walking down this street had better watch out. They're going to bump into one of the biggest birds that ever existed. And it will do more than ruffle a few feathers. Those massively powerful legs can break bones and worse. But hey, at least it won't eat the passersby! Scientists believe it was a herbivore. This ostrich-like bird lived on the island of Madagascar and couldn't fly, but it grew so big because it had plenty of fruit to eat in the forests and no predators to bother it.

In fact, its only predator seems to have been humans. Scientists think humans hunted the bird to extinction in the seventeenth or eighteenth century. You can see why. Elephant bird eggs were bigger than footballs and would have made an eggstraordinary thirty omelettes. And there would have been plenty of meat on the bird itself. It is sad to see such an imposing creature go. But scientists have been able to extract DNA from an elephant bird's egg, so maybe one day it will be seen walking down the road again.

ELEPHANT BIRD
LIVED
Madagascar, from about 40,000 years ago until the seventeenth century
HEIGHT
Up to 10 feet (3 m)
WEIGHT
Up to 1,100 pounds (500 kg)

VERY EGGSPENSIVE
Intact elephant birds' eggs are very rare and valuable. In 2013, the London auctioneers Christie's sold an egg for a whopping $101,813. That turned out to be a cracking sale.

TIMELINE

DEINOGALERIX

Named after the Greek for "terrible shrew"

On Gargano island, the only predator that might have threatened *Deinogalerix* was the gigantic prehistoric barn owl *Tyto gigantea*. It had a wingspan of around 6 feet, 2 inches (1.9 m).

ARTHROPLEURA

Named after the Greek for "jointed ribs"

Fossil hunters have found lots of preserved footprints of *Arthropleura*, as well as fossilized body parts. They show that the giant millipede moved quickly across forest floors, swerving to avoid trees and rocks.

BEELZEBUFO

Named after Beelzebub (the devil), and *bufo*, Latin for toad

Devil frog fossils were first found in 1993, but it took 15 years and 75 more fossils to work out what it looked like.

MEGANEURA

Named after the Greek for "large-nerved"

Meganeura lived in the great forests and swamps of the late Carboniferous period. As plants collapsed into the water, they were buried underground and eventually turned into coal.

TITANOBOA

Meaning "titanic boa" or huge boa (a snake of the Boidae family)

What did *Titanoboa* eat? It lived in swampy jungles in South America, so crocodiles were a likely dish. It may also have eaten giant turtles such as *Carbonemys*, but the 5-foot, 6-inch (1.7 m) shell might have taken some digesting!

MEGALANIA

Named after the Greek for "great roamer"

Megalania is about twice the size of the Komodo dragon, which lives on islands in Indonesia and can be up to 10 feet (3 m) long. *Megalania* is also related to the Komodo dragon—both are from the varanid family of lizards.

CASTOROIDES

From the Greek name Castor, "he who excels"

Why *Castoroides* went extinct about 10,000 years ago is unknown. This is when humans arrived in North America, and they might have hunted them to extinction. But some scientists think the plants *Castoroides* ate were also declining.

ELEPHANT BIRD

The elephant bird looks like an oversized ostrich, but its closest living relative is the chicken-sized kiwi of New Zealand, which is also flightless. The elephant bird —the heaviest bird ever— may have had a kiwi-like ancestor.

JOSEPHOARTIGASIA

Named after José Artigas, the founding father of Uruguay, where the first specimen was found

Scientists think *Josephoartigasia* used its incisors not just for biting but also for digging in the ground for food and warding off predators.

DWARF ELEPHANTS

These early elephants are an example of insular dwarfism, when large mammals living on islands become smaller. Dwarf elephants are distinct from pygmy elephants, which still exist in Borneo and Africa and are a larger species.

4 MILLION YEARS AGO

350 YEARS AGO

UNCOVERING THE PAST

The scientists who study prehistoric animals and plants are known as paleontologists. To find out about life in the past, they search for and study fossils. Fossils are simply animal and plant remains that have been preserved in rocks.

Fossils prove an animal existed, but they don't prove that it is extinct! For instance, many fossils have been found of the giant ape *Gigantopithecus,* and most scientists think it died out 100,000 years ago. But some people claim *Gigantopithecus* still exists—people just call it the Yeti or Big Foot these days!

However, there is no proof of this. Scientists believe *Gigantopithecus* walked on four feet like its orangutan relatives, while people who claim to have seen the Yeti or Big Foot say it walks on two feet. What's more, Big Foot is supposed to live in the northwestern United States, and *Gigantopithecus* fossils have only been found in Asia.

So how do paleontologists dig out fossils? It's not exactly high-tech. It involves simple tools and a little elbow grease. For breaking up big rocks around the fossil, paleontologists might use a rock hammer or a hammer and chisel. When they get closer, a digging knife, a trowel, or a steel point comes in handy. Sometimes, paleontologists make their own tools—out of bamboo, for example.

While digging, they use a brush to remove dirt from the fossil so they can see what they are doing. It can be a long process, but the important thing is to get the fossil out in one piece. And if they fail, some glue comes in handy!

Anyone can find a fossil!

You don't need to be a professional paleontologist to discover a prehistoric creature. Many have been found by children. In 2015, a young girl discovered the fossil of a 25-million-year-old flightless bird on Vancouver Island in Canada. It was a new species of Plotopterid, a group of penguin-like birds. Perhaps the greatest fossil hunter of all was 12-year-old Mary Anning, who found the first complete skeleton of the marine reptile *Ichthyosaurus* on the south coast of England in 1811. You can begin your own searches by joining a fossil-hunting group or organization.

Fossil of a trilobite, a hard-shelled sea creature that lived over 520 million years ago

INDEX

The Author
Matthew Rake lives in London, in the United Kingdom, and has worked in publishing for more than twenty years. He has written on a wide variety of topics for adults as well as children, including science, sports, and the arts.

The Illustrator
Award-winning illustrator Simon Mendez combines his love of nature and drawing by working as an illustrator with a focus on scientific and natural subjects. He paints on a wide variety of themes but mainly concentrates on portraits and animal subjects. He lives in the United Kingdom.